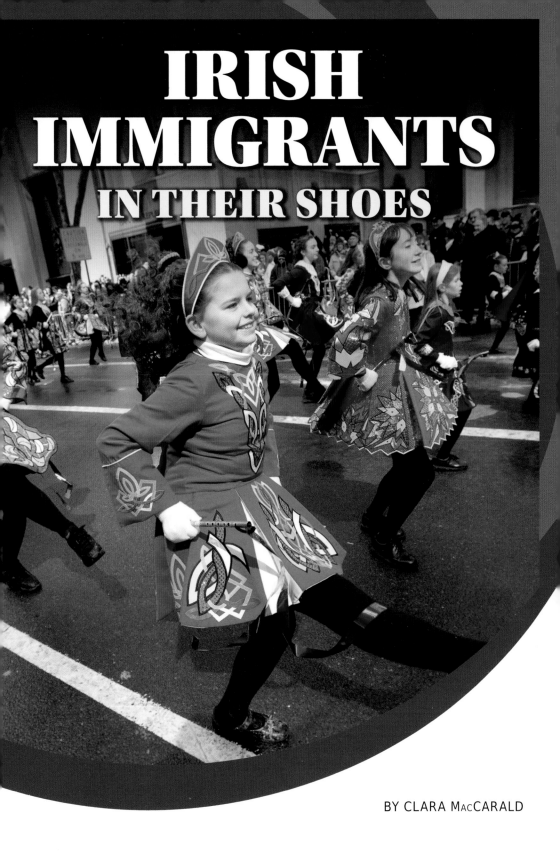

IRISH IMMIGRANTS
IN THEIR SHOES

BY CLARA MacCARALD

Published by The Child's World®
1980 Lookout Drive • Mankato, MN 56003-1705
800-599-READ • www.childsworld.com

Content Consultant: Cian T. McMahon, PhD, Assistant Professor of History, University of Nevada, Las Vegas

Photographs ©: Shiho Fukada/AP Images, cover, 1; Thomas Leitch/Library of Congress, 6; North Wind Picture Archives, 8, 11, 17, 22, 25; Everett Historical/Shutterstock Images, 12; Red Line Editorial, 14; John Rubens Smith/John Rubens Smith Collection/Library of Congress, 18; Liszt Collection/Heritage Images/Glow Images, 21; Dan Hallman/Invision/AP Images, 26; Paul A. Hebert/Invision/AP Images, 28

ISBN 9781503820289
LCCN 2016960927

Printed in the United States of America
PA02338

ABOUT THE AUTHOR

Clara MacCarald is a freelance writer with a master's degree in biology who writes educational books for children. She has also written about news and science for local publications in central New York. She belongs to the National Association of Science Writers and the Society of Children's Book Writers and Illustrators.

TABLE OF CONTENTS

FAST FACTS

Important Years

- Irish immigration to the United States was at its highest between 1820 and 1920.
- **Potato blight** caused a **famine** in Ireland from 1845 to 1855.

Important Numbers

- From 1820 to 1920, nearly 5 million Irish people left for the United States.
- During the potato famine, approximately 1.5 million Irish immigrants fled to the United States.

Reasons for Irish Immigration

- Some Irish immigrants hoped for better job opportunities.
- Many Irish immigrants fled famine and poor living conditions due to the potato blight in Ireland.

TIMELINE

1541: Henry VIII, the Protestant king of England, declares himself king of Ireland.

1798: A rebellion in Ireland fails, and some of its supporters flee to the United States.

1825: Irish immigrants and other laborers finish construction of the Erie Canal, which links New York City to the Great Lakes.

1834: An anti-Irish mob burns down a home for Catholic nuns near Boston, Massachusetts.

1845: The potato blight arrives in Ireland, causing famine.

1855: The decade of the famine ends.

1861: The U.S. Civil War (1861–1865) begins, with Irish immigrants fighting on both sides.

1863: Irish laborers participate in **draft** riots in New York City.

1922: Most of Ireland gains independence from the United Kingdom.

1960: Americans elect John F. Kennedy, a **descendant** of Irish immigrants, as president.

Chapter 1

COLONIAL IRISH

In the fall of 1734, six-year-old Robert Witherspoon and his extended family boarded a ship in Belfast, Ireland. Tall sails towered overhead. Like hundreds of thousands of Irish, the Witherspoons were headed to Great Britain's American colonies. The passengers would live below the decks during their long journey across the Atlantic Ocean.

◀ **In the 1700s, ships had tall sails and took weeks to cross the ocean.**

Robert's family was Scotch-Irish, and they belonged to the Presbyterian Church. But Ireland's laws supported the Church of Ireland. That meant people who practiced other religions, such as Presbyterians and Catholics, could not hold government jobs. They were not allowed to teach in schools or attend universities. And they often struggled to make a living. Most Presbyterians and Catholics rented land rather than owned it. The cost of rent often increased. During some years, harvests failed and many people starved.

Robert's family was headed to the colony of South Carolina. There they hoped to find religious freedom and land to farm. But first they had to get there. Robert's grandmother died after they left Belfast. Storms on the open ocean stirred up strong waves that tossed the ship about. Water began leaking through the hull. Robert listened day and night as the ship's pumps pushed the water back out to sea.

After two months at sea, the ship sailed into Charleston, South Carolina. Beyond the docks stood storehouses and grand buildings. Horses pulled carts through the sandy streets, which were laid out neatly. Robert and his family were grateful to reach the colonial town. But it was only the first stop on their journey.

Robert's family stayed in Charleston for several weeks. Finally, the time came for the survivors to travel to their new home. They planned to move inland. To do so, they boarded a small boat and traveled along rivers. The settlers packed farming tools in their boat. They loaded enough grain and meat to feed themselves through the next year while they began farming their new land.

The boat, open to the cold air, moved up the river. Woodlands stood all around. At night, Robert and many of the others went ashore and spent the night in a barn. His father had gone ahead to build their new house. The next day, his new neighbors helped carry children and supplies through swampy woods covered with frost. Finally, his family reached the house his father built.

The small house had dirt walls and looked like a hut for storing potatoes. The family's spirit sank. "Father gave us all the comfort he could by telling us that we would get all these trees cut down," Robert later wrote. "And in a short time there would be plenty of inhabitants so that we could see from house to house."[1] The day grew late, and wolves howled all around.

The settlement slowly grew. People continued to leave Ireland because of bad harvests and high rents. The Witherspoon family knew they had been lucky to afford the trip to America. In general, Presbyterians in Ireland had more money than Catholics.

◀ **Many Irish immigrants lived in simple cabins with walls made of earth, just as they had in Ireland.**

Many immigrants could not pay for the voyage. These people became **indentured servants**. To pay back the money for their ticket, they agreed to work without a wage for several years.

Rosanna Stuart was one of the many Irish indentured servants in the American colonies. And like most indentured servants, she had a difficult life. One day she ran away with clothes that belonged to the woman she worked for. Later, she was found in a house for poor people in Philadelphia, Pennsylvania. She explained her reasoning for running away. "The hardships I suffered (were) so great," she said. "The winter before I ran away I had no bed . . . but the cold earth to lie on."[2]

In more heavily settled areas, colonists often made the Irish feel unwelcome. Many Protestants didn't like the religion or manners of the Irish. They thought the Irish were out of control. As a result, many free Irish settled in the backwoods of Great Britain's American colonies. Throughout the next century, Irish immigrants struggled to be accepted as equals by other Americans.

In the 1700s, many Irish immigrants lived in the countryside ▶ because they did not feel welcome in cities.

Chapter 2

THE GREAT FAMINE

In July 1846, Father Theobald Mathew set out from the south of Ireland to Dublin in the east. Mathew often traveled as part of his work. Green potato stalks filled the fields he passed. A small field of potatoes could feed a family of six for a year. Although their fields were full, the people were very poor. Near the fields stood mud cabins, broken fences, and roofless barns.

◄ **The Great Famine resulted in approximately one million deaths in Ireland.**

After a week, Mathew headed back. A deathly odor hung over the land. It was the sign of a fungus called potato blight. Blight had appeared the year before, but now it spread everywhere. People sat on garden fences, wailing. Rotting vegetation filled their fields. A peasant remembered the scene in Sligo, Ireland. "You could begin to see the tops of the stalks lying over as if the life was gone out of them," he said. "And that was the beginning of the great trouble and famine that destroyed Ireland."[3]

Below ground, the potatoes oozed with rot. Even potatoes that looked healthy fell apart in storage. Starving people formed angry crowds in the cities and countryside. Feeling hopeless, hundreds of thousands of people fled to the United States.

In the spring of 1847, on a ship called the *India*, a man shouted out as he spotted land. The *India* had been at sea for more than a month. The hills of Staten Island, New York, slowly came into view. Passengers cheered and fell to their knees on the ship's wet wooden floor. Like other famine ships, the *India* was packed with weak and hungry Irish fleeing the famine. Many on the *India* had **typhus**. Some had died on the journey.

The next day, smaller boats took the passengers to the docks. Officials feared the Irish would spread illness throughout the city.

So the passengers had to go to the Staten Island **quarantine** station. After a long walk down the pier, the new arrivals passed a tall brick wall. Then they arrived at the cluster of stone buildings where they would live for the next month.

IRISH IMMIGRATION TO THE UNITED STATES

Time Period	Number of Immigrants
Colonial Times (before 1783)	400,000–600,000
Early Years of the United States (1783-1815)	100,000–150,000
Before the Great Famine (1816-1844)	800,000–1,000,000
During the Great Famine (1845-1855)	1,800,000
After the Great Famine (1856-1921)	3,100,000
After Irish Independence (1922-1950)	260,000

Four weeks passed, and their time in quarantine was finally over. The immigrants were free to enter the city. They took a boat to the city docks. After crewmembers threw a rope to the dock and tied it up, men from the city jumped aboard. They grabbed the passengers' bags, trying to convince people to stay at a particular inn.

Many of the immigrants were too poor to leave New York City. They had no choice but to live in dark, dirty cellars. Disease spread easily in these places. Danger also came from other Irish, some of whom formed gangs to support each other. Work was dangerous, too, because there were few safety regulations. Laborers spent long hours moving goods, constructing buildings, working with stone, or sewing in factories.

Back in Ireland, the Great Famine was still causing terrible suffering. A man named John Jackson asked his wife Sally if she would like to see her sister, who was living in the United States. At first, Sally leaped with joy. But then she thought about the family members she would have to leave behind in Ireland. "My mother," she said. "What is she to do?"[4] John said they would be of more use to her mother in the United States, where they could make money and send it to Ireland. Tears ran down Sally's face.

John and Sally eventually landed in New Orleans, Louisiana. As in other port cities, poor immigrants filled dirty apartments.

Sick and weak Irish immigrants sometimes crawled through the streets.

John and Sally became two of the unlucky ones. On the ship, John had cared for a sick friend. "Three days before I landed I took the fever off him myself," John wrote. "I lay for five weeks, and then Sally took ill."[5]

A wagon carried Sally to a hospital, where she later died. John spent weeks recovering from his illness. Finally, he managed to start work as a miner, although his sorrow was still great. In time, he saved enough money to send some to Sally's mother and other family in Ireland. He found success in the United States, but the price had been terribly high.

Immigrants often left Ireland with nothing, and not all achieved success. In many cases, they stayed poor and suffered **discrimination**. For example, some individuals and companies did not want to hire Irish Catholics. In the 1850s, native-born Americans formed a political movement to oppose immigrants, especially the Irish.

Anger sometimes brought Irish immigrants together. They blamed England for not stopping the famine. Irish neighborhoods united to support each other and find pride in being Irish.

Immigrants often arrived with very few belongings. ▶

Chapter 3

WORKING FOR
A BETTER LIFE

A nn McNabb longed to leave Ireland. But it was the 1850s, and she had very little money. One day she received money from her sister Tilly, who lived in Philadelphia. Ann used the money to buy a ticket to the United States. She boarded a tall ship called the *Mary Jane* and said good-bye to her homeland. For eight weeks, Ann lived in the dirty space below the ship's deck.

Some of the passengers ran out of food, but others shared what they had. The trip was free of hunger or fever.

Poor immigrants crowded into Philadelphia, just as they did in other American port cities. Expensive horse-drawn buses moved through the main streets. But shabby houses filled side streets. Renters packed themselves into small apartments.

When Ann reached Philadelphia, she felt lucky to join her sister. Tilly worked as a housekeeper for a wealthy family. Servants received a free room and free food. Back in Ireland, the sisters' family had eaten mostly potatoes. But now Tilly taught Ann the American ways of washing, cooking, and baking.

After many years of hard work, Ann and Tilly saved enough money to rent a house of their own. The house was small but nice. They sent money so their parents could pay for passage to Philadelphia. "To think of mother having a parlor and marble steps and a bell," Ann marveled. Their parents arrived on a steamer one night. "We had supper for them and the house all lighted up. Well, you ought to have seen mother's old face!"[6]

When the U.S. Civil War started in 1861, many Irish Americans fought for the North, also called the Union. By serving in the war, immigrants hoped to be taken more seriously as Americans.

But other Irish Americans fought for the South. As the war dragged on, the Union started a draft because the army needed more soldiers. Many hated the draft. They also hated the idea of freeing the slaves. Many Irish immigrants feared that the freed slaves would take their jobs.

"The different kinds of (food) that we have on the table every day are beef, pork, lamb, chicken, ducks, turkeys, veal, sweet potatoes and Irish potatoes, cabbage, onions, beets, tomatoes, corn, beans, peas, cranberries, apples, pies, puddings, and many other things."

— *Mary Garvey, an Irish American immigrant writing to her mother in 1850*[7]

On a hot July morning in 1863, Irish immigrants filled the streets in New York City. Their numbers swelled as people left factories and workshops. The crowd surrounded the building where officials were picking names for the draft.

Rioters threw stones through the windows and set the building on fire. As the fury spread through the city, rioters also started attacking black people. Many Irish immigrants saw black people as a threat to their well-being.

▲ **Irish Americans cause destruction during a draft riot in 1863.**

Four days later, Union troops ended the riot. Hundreds of people were dead, and New Yorkers were stunned by the mob's behavior.

Chapter 4

FROM IRISH IMMIGRANTS TO IRISH AMERICANS

L eonora Barry left Ireland as a young child during the famine years. As an adult, she found a job at a garment factory. But after a week on the job, she was shocked at how little she had earned. Like many other Irish immigrants, she started trying to change factory conditions.

◄ Workers in the late 1800s often dealt with low wages and dangerous conditions.

In 1887, Barry traveled to Paterson, New Jersey. On a normal day, the city's many factories would have been humming with activity. But when Barry arrived, the factories were silent. Hundreds of people were at home instead of at their jobs. They were on **strike**.

As part of a labor group, Barry had been traveling around New Jersey to meet with women workers. Everywhere she went, she asked about the conditions of the factories. She found women working for low wages. They toiled in crowded rooms with little air. Many factories were very severe about their workers' conduct. "A fine is imposed for eating, laughing, singing, or talking," Barry wrote about one factory. "If not inside the gate in the morning when the whistle stops blowing, (a worker) is locked out until half-past seven . . . and many other rules equally . . . unjust."[8]

In Paterson, Barry talked to the inactive workers. Before the United States outlawed child labor, children as young as five were put to work making clothes. The child workers in Paterson had gone on strike to ask for 5 cents more a day. But instead of raising wages, the factory had locked the door and kept all the workers out.

"They have this home here for working girls . . . there must be nearly 200. . . . They charge from three to six dollars a week for room and board. At half past six every morning they ring a large bell to wake the girls up, again at seven for breakfast, and then for dinner and supper."

—Josephine, an Irish immigrant, in 1906[9]

Barry continued to travel around the country to report on these and other struggles. She encouraged workers to come together and ask for better conditions. In 1890, Barry married and left her labor work. However, she continued to work toward improving the lives of women and children.

Thanks partially to the work of Barry and others, the lives of many Irish immigrants started to improve in the early 1900s. They worked better jobs. The children of Irish immigrants grew more successful, but many Irish communities were still very poor. New immigrants were arriving from places such as eastern Europe. To many Americans, the Irish seemed less strange by comparison.

In 1963, U.S. president John F. Kennedy stood in front of a crowd in Ireland. "This is not the land of my birth," he told them.

▲ **Child workers make twine in the late 1800s.**

"But it is the land for which I hold the greatest affection."[10]
Kennedy was the descendant of Irish immigrants. For many,
Kennedy's election was a sign that the Irish were truly accepted
as Americans.

Chapter 5

ACTING AMERICAN

Jason O'Mara was beating himself up—literally. His high school rugby career in Ireland was taking a toll on his body. He was getting to the point where he had to give up the sport. Jason was a good student. But he needed something to replace the thrill he got from playing rugby. He found that thrill on the stage.

Jason acted in high school and through his time at Trinity College in Dublin, Ireland. That led to more work outside of school.

He was even nominated for an award at the 2002 Irish Theatre Awards. Jason felt inspired to try his luck in California. "Theater work led me to more work and then to me moving to the States," he said. "I've been very fortunate in that I love what I do."[11]

Jason was already familiar with American television. As a boy, he grew up watching the old *Batman* TV series from the 1960s. But American life was totally new. Though Dublin was a big city, it felt safe and familiar. The hustle and bustle of life in Los Angeles, California, took a lot of getting used to.

On the set of one of his first U.S. television shows, Jason found someone to help him through. He was cast in a show starring actress Paige Turco. The two fell in love, and they married in 2003. A year later, they welcomed a son.

Jason's career was also taking off. He landed regular roles on several TV shows. In 2008, he achieved his first starring role in a crime drama show. The show lasted for only one season. Audiences saw that Jason was a rising star.

By 2009, Jason had been living in the United States for several years. He decided it was time to officially become a U.S. citizen. After an interview and a test on American history, Jason received his U.S. passport. "That was a very proud moment," he said.[12]

But Jason hasn't totally forgotten his Irish roots. Sunday roast is a tradition in Ireland, and the O'Mara family has carried that on. Paige also learned to make traditional Irish favorites such as Yorkshire pudding and soda bread.

Jason's talent took him from Ireland to the United States. He wasn't one to shy away from taking risks to get where he wanted to be. "Sometimes the things that scare me are the things I'm drawn to," he said. "In order to live a full life, sometimes you have to do things that scare you."[13]

THINK ABOUT IT

- What were some of the different reasons Irish immigrants left Ireland? Did some people have more than one reason?
- What kinds of discrimination did Irish immigrants face in America? How did they respond?
- Do you think most Irish immigrants found what they were looking for in America? Why or why not?

◀ **Jason and Paige attend a movie premiere in 2013.**

GLOSSARY

descendant (di-SEN-dunt): A descendant is a person's children, grandchildren, and so on. U.S. president John F. Kennedy was the descendant of Irish immigrants.

discrimination (dis-krim-i-NAY-shun): Discrimination is unfair behavior toward someone because of a difference such as race or gender. Some Irish immigrants looking for work faced discrimination.

draft (DRAFT): A draft is a system that requires people to serve in the military. Some Irish immigrants were upset about the draft during the U.S. Civil War.

famine (FAM-in): A famine is a serious lack of food in an area. Many potato plants began to die in 1845, leading to a famine in Ireland.

indentured servants (in-DEN-cherd SUR-vunts): Indentured servants are people who have agreed to work for a certain amount of time without pay. Some people who could not pay for their trip to the American colonies became indentured servants.

potato blight (puh-TAY-toh BLITE): Potato blight is a disease caused by a fungus that destroys potato plants. Potato blight caused the Great Famine.

quarantine (KWOR-un-teen): A quarantine is a way of keeping people, animals, or plants apart from others to control the spread of disease. New York City had a quarantine station to try to stop disease from spreading through the city.

strike (STRYK): A strike is when workers refuse to work until they get what they are asking for. The workers went on strike for better pay.

typhus (TY-fus): Typhus is a disease that causes rashes, headaches, and fevers. Some people on the famine ships caught typhus.

SOURCE NOTES

1. Kerby A. Miller et al., eds. *Irish Immigrants in the Land of Canaan: Letters and Memoirs from Colonial and Revolutionary America, 1675–1815.* New York, NY: Oxford University Press, 2003. Print. 138.

2. Ibid. 260–261.

3. Kerby A. Miller. *Emigrants and Exiles: Ireland and the Irish Exodus to North America.* New York, NY: Oxford University Press, 1985. Print. 282.

4. John Jackson. "Letter from John Jackson (Brother-in-Law), Monaghan [Ireland], 17 February 1848." *Immigrant Letters.* Provincial Archives of New Brunswick, n.d. Web. 24 Jan. 2017.

5. John Jackson. "Transcript of Letter from John Jackson (Brother-in-Law), St. Lewis [St. Louis], 12 February 1850." *Immigrant Letters.* Provincial Archives of New Brunswick, n.d. Web. 24 Jan. 2017.

6. Hamilton Holt, ed. *The Life Stories of Undistinguished Americans as Told by Themselves.* New York, NY: J. Potts & Company, 1906. 147. *Google Books.* Web. 24 Jan. 2017.

7. Mary Garvey. "Letter from Mary Garvey, Irish Immigrant, to Her Mother, October 24, 1850." *New Jersey Digital Highway.* New Jersey Digital Highway, n.d. Web. 24 Jan. 2017.

8. Lenora M. Barry. "Barry's Report to the Knights of Labor, 1887." *New Jersey Women's History.* Alice Paul Institute, n.d. Web. 24 Jan. 2017.

9. "Letter from Cousin Josephine, Boston, Massachusetts, to John McCarthy, 14 May 1906." *Immigrant Letters.* Provincial Archives of New Brunswick, n.d. Web. 24 Jan. 2017.

10. "A Journey Home: John F. Kennedy in Ireland." *John F. Kennedy Presidential Library and Museum.* John F. Kennedy Presidential Library and Museum, n.d. Web. 24 Jan. 2017.

11. Sean Abrams. "Outfitted: Jason O'Mara." *Maxim.* Maxim Media, 25 June 2015. Web. 24 Jan. 2017.

12. Thelma Adams. "Jason O'Mara on Risk Taking and Becoming an American Citizen." *Parade.* AMG/Parade, 14 Jan. 2012. Web. 24 Jan. 2017.

13. Ibid.

TO LEARN MORE

Books

Heaney, Shane. *The Scotch-Irish Immigration to America: Economic Hardship in Ireland (1603–1775)*. New York, NY: PowerKids Press, 2016.

Lyons, Mary E., editor. *Feed the Children First: Irish Memories of the Great Hunger*. New York, NY: Atheneum Books for Young Readers, 2012.

O'Donoghue, Sean. *The Disaster of the Irish Potato Famine: Irish Immigrants Arrive in America (1845–1850)*. New York, NY: PowerKids Press, 2016.

Web Sites

Visit our Web site for links about Irish immigrants:
childsworld.com/links

Note to Parents, Teachers, and Librarians: We routinely verify our Web links to make sure they are safe and active sites. So encourage your readers to check them out!

INDEX